Settlements

FRED MARTIN

First published in Great Britain by Heinemann Library
Halley Court, Jordan Hill, Oxford OX2 8EJ
a division of Reed Educational & Professional Publishing Ltd

MELBOURNE AUCKLAND
FLORENCE PRAGUE MADRID ATHENS
SINGAPORE TOKYO CHICAGO SAO PAULO
PORTSMOUTH NH MEXICO
IBADAN GABORONE JOHANNESBURG
KAMPALA NAIROBI

Designed by Artistix
Originated by Dot Gradations Ltd., South Woodham Ferrers
Printed in the UK by Jarrold Book Printing Ltd., Thetford

00 99 98 97 96
10 9 8 7 6 5 4 3 2 1

ISBN 0 431 06432 6

British Library Cataloguing in Publication Data

Martin, Fred, 1948 –
 Settlements. – (Themes in geography)
 1. Land settlement – Juvenile literature 2. Human settlements –
 Juvenile literature
 I. Title II. Series
 307.1'4

Acknowledgements
The Publishers would like to thank the following for permission to reproduce photographs.

Ace Photo Library/Mauritius: p.23. Ace Photo Library/Michael Harding: p.28. Ace Photo Library/Nowrocki Stock: p.10. Ace Photo Library/Paul Thompson: p.37. Barnaby's Picture Library: p.32. Bruce Coleman: p.25, p.27. Bruce Coleman/Dr Charles Henneghien: p.6, p.15. Bruce Coleman/John Shaw: p.38. Frank Spooner/Gamma/V Leloup/Figaro: p.16. Frank Spooner/Steve Margan: p.41. Fred Martin: p.8, p.24, p.34, p.35. London Aerial Photo Library: p.20. Magnum/Chris Steele: p.42. Magnum/Dennis Stock: p.13. Magnum/Ian Berry: p.9. Magnum/Jones Nachtwey: p.43. Magnum/Steve Arnold: p.29. Magnum/Stuart Franklin: p.26. Pictor International: p.44. Pictor Uniphoto: p.19. Rex Features/Robert Judges: p.31. Robert Harding Picture Library: p.12. Robert Harding Picture Library/Adam Woolfitt: p.18. Robert Harding Picture Library/Christopher Rennie: p.30. Robert Harding Picture Library/Philip Craven: p.7. Spectrum: p.17, p.21. Still Pictures/Herbert Giradet: p.11. Still Pictures/John Maier: p.40. Still Pictures/Mark Edwards: p.39, p.45. Still Pictures/Oliver Gillie: p.5. Telegraph Colour Library/Karin Slade: p.22. The Image Bank/Burton McNealy: p.33. Tony Stone/Bruce Forste: p.36. Tony Stone Images/Ian Murphy: p.4.

Cover photograph reproduced with permission of The Image Bank.

Our thanks to Clare Boast, Sutherland Primary School, Stoke on Trent, for her comments in the preparation of this book.

Every effort has been made to contact copyright holders of any material reproduced in this book. Any omissions will be rectified in subsequent printings if notice is given to the Publisher.

Contents

Small settlements

Almost everybody lives in a **settlement**. This means they live in one place. The only people who do not live like this are called **nomads**. They travel from place to place and never settle down.

Isolated settlements

A settlement can be any size. A farm house is an **isolated settlement**. This means it is on its own. In Australia, a cattle station is usually an isolated settlement. It can be a hundred miles from the next nearest settlement. In the UK, isolated farm houses are never further than a few miles from other farms or houses.

Why did villages form?

A small group of houses is called a **hamlet**. It becomes a village when there are a few more houses and some other buildings and services.

Villages usually began because people needed to live near to each other. They helped each other grow crops and raise animals. This is still a common reason why people in some countries live together in villages.

A village in Zambia where people make their living by farming.

Everyone takes a share in the work, including children.

A good site

The place where a settlement is built is called its site. In the past, a settlement's site had to be carefully chosen. There had to be a water supply from a river, lake or spring. A sheltered site was better than one that was exposed to strong wind and cold temperatures.

Some settlements were built on the top of a hill or inside the bend of a river. These were sites that were easier to defend.

Most settlements have grown far beyond their first site. The reasons for choosing the site are usually not important any more.

A small settlement in Cumbria.

The settlement was built in the shelter of the valley bottom.

There was a water supply from mountain streams.

Village services

In the past, most villages in Britain had a blacksmith's workshop, a mill, a bakery and church. These are examples of different types of services.

Today, there are not so many different services. Most people buy their bread in a supermarket. Fewer blacksmiths are needed because most people own cars. A village church is still useful for worship and special church services. Some villages are lucky enough to have a local school for village children.

Did you know?

Most settlements in the UK were started before the Norman Conquest in 1066. They were built by Celts, Saxons or Vikings.

One of the UK's newest villages is being built at Poundbury near Dorchester in Dorset. This is a village with 3000 houses and other services. The village is on land owned by Prince Charles.

Going to market

A street market in Mali.

Women have brought food from their farms to sell in the town.

Many towns began because some people had things to sell that others needed to buy. The best way to do this was to meet in one place on one day every week.

The first markets

Most old towns have a market street or square. Farmers brought their animals and food to sell. Townspeople and farmers bought what they needed at the market.

In medieval times in England, a village could not become a market town unless it had permission from the king or queen. Permission was given in a **charter**.

Having a charter meant that a tax could be collected from everyone trading in the market. This bought money into the town and helped make some people rich.

Every area only needed one market town. The place chosen was usually the one that was most central, or was easiest to get to. Some market towns grew up near a castle where people felt safe.

Earning money

Selling food on market day is one way farmers in poor countries earn money. Most food is grown to be eaten by the farmer's family. This is known as **subsistence farming**. Any surplus is sold to buy more seed, animals or to pay for improvements to the farm. This helps improve their standard of living.

The need to buy and sell

In the UK, food markets are still held in the larger cities, starting very early in the morning. Shop and restaurant owners go there to buy food such as fresh fruit and vegetables. These are sold on to customers later in the day.

Shopping markets

Other types of market are also held. Some of these take place on open spaces in the centre of a town or on large areas of empty land. People then buy all sorts of goods from **traders** who travel from town to town. They move from market day in one town to a different market day in another town.

Did you know?

For 300 years, Covent Garden in central London was the fruit and vegetable market for the city. In 1974, it was moved to a new site with more space. The old market building is now used for shopping and leisure.

Market day in Norwich, Norfolk.

The city was given its market charter in 1158.

Stalls are put up in the market square for the day.

A wide range of food and other goods are sold by market traders.

Mining and factories

Towns always have a reason for existing in a particular place. Some have grown because a large number of people were needed in one place. This is true for mining and making goods in a factory.

Mining villages

Large-scale mining and quarrying for coal and iron ore began during the Industrial Revolution. In the UK, this lasted from about 1750 to 1900. Steam engines that used coal were invented. New ways were found to melt iron by burning coal.

Villages for miners were built in **coalfield** areas and near iron ore. Many of these villages are still there even though the coal mines closed down long ago.

Towns for miners

Large numbers of people are still needed to work in some mines and quarries, though machines now do much of the work. When a **mineral** such as oil or uranium is found in a remote place, a new mining settlement has to be built. Some of these are temporary workers camps. Others are more permanent **settlements** for miners and their families.

If the mineral runs out or is no longer needed, these settlements can become **'ghost towns'**. The buildings may remain, but the people move on to new jobs and new towns.

An old coal mine near Blaenavon in south Wales.

Mining villages were built in the valleys of south Wales during the Industrial Revolution.

The pit was closed in 1980 and is now a tourist attraction.

Factory towns

During the Industrial Revolution, the first large factories were built in the UK. These new **manufacturing industries** used machines powered by steam engines so goods could be made much more quickly than before.

Some factory jobs still had to be done by hand. Workers were also needed to operate the machinery. People moved from country areas to factory towns to do these jobs.

Sometimes a special town was built just for the workers. This is what happened at the Cadbury chocolate factory in Bourneville near Birmingham. In most places workers had to find their own homes. Rows of terraced houses were built quickly for renting to factory workers.

The best place

Industrial towns have grown where factories can get the **raw materials** they need. Pittsburgh in the USA was near coal and iron ore so it became a centre for making iron and steel.

Some towns have grown because several factories needed to be near each other. For example, parts made for a car come together from different factories to be made into the car. Birmingham in the UK and Detroit in the USA became centres for making cars and car parts.

Bradford, an industrial town in Yorkshire, has a history of making woollen goods in factories.

Did you know?

In 1769, Thomas Watt invented one of the first steam engines that could power machinery.

Less than 100 people lived in the farming village of Middlesborough in 1800. By 1851, a railway, port and industrial development had made it a town with 7500 people.

The capital city

The Capitol building in Washington DC, USA.

The politicians who govern the USA have met in this building since 1800.

The President of the USA lives in a building in Washington DC called the White House.

Every country has a city that is unique in one special way. This is the **capital city** where the country's **government** does its work, and where the leader usually lives.

Cities for administration

The work done by a government is called **administration**. **Politicians** make decisions about how hospitals, schools and the armed forces are run. They also decide on how much money people should pay in taxes. In the UK, politicians meet in the Houses of Parliament.

Government offices

Office workers called **civil servants** also work in the capital city. They help the politicians do their work and make sure that the government's decisions are carried out.

In the USA, about 400,000 civil servants work in the capital city, Washington DC. In the UK, thousands of civil servants work in different government departments. These departments in London are called **Ministries**. Some government work is done in other cities such as in Newcastle, Cardiff and Glasgow.

Choosing a capital city

Some of the world's largest cities are capital cities, for example, Mexico City. The capital city is often the largest city in the country. London and Paris are the largest cities in the UK and France.

Some capital cities are not the largest. Canberra, the capital city of Australia, is twelve times smaller than the better-known city, Sydney.

A few cities have been specially built to be the capital. Brasilia in Brazil and Islamabad in Pakistan are two of these.

In the middle

A capital city is best in a place where most people in the country can get to it. The word **location** describes where a place is.

Some capital cities, such as Madrid in Spain, are near the centre of their country. Others, such as Washington DC, are nowhere near the centre. There are often historic reasons for this. Some countries have changed their size and shape during their history. For example, Moscow was in the centre of Russia when the country was much smaller. Now it is far from the centre of a much larger country.

Did you know?

A competition was held to find the best design for Brasilia. Building work began on the winning design in 1960.

Brasilia is the capital city of Brazil.

The capital used to be Rio de Janeiro but this city became too crowded.

Holiday towns

Going on holiday often means visiting another town. A town that is a popular place for people to visit is called a **resort**. Seaside resorts are some of the world's most popular towns to visit.

The first seaside resorts

People have not always taken holidays by the sea. They only started doing this in 1754 when a doctor said that bathing in sea water was good for people's health.

At first, only rich people could go somewhere for a holiday. After trains were invented, more people were able to get to the seaside. Towns such as Blackpool and Weston-super-Mare soon became popular holiday spots for workers in the **industrial towns** and cities.

History and tourists

As early as the late eighteenth century, people went on holiday to drink the local natural mineral water. This was supposed to be good for the health. People went to Bath, Cheltenham and other **spa towns**.

The Roman baths in the city of Bath.

Old buildings and the city's Roman history make it a popular city for tourists.

Towns for tourists

Many buildings in modern holiday towns are specially for the visitors. There are hotels and other types of accommodation. Shops sell souvenirs. Restaurants and leisure facilities are also built.

People in the town take jobs in the **tourist industry**. These towns are very busy during the holiday season then become quiet again for the rest of the year.

The spread of tourism

There are now holiday resorts in places that used to be hard to get to. In the future, it looks as if tourists will be visiting places that are even further away from home. Already, there are new resorts in Africa and Asia. These places are now easy to reach by air from countries in Europe.

Fort Lauderdale in Florida, USA.

This seaside resort is popular because of the warm temperatures both in summer and in winter. This attracts people from cities further north where the weather is not so hot.

Did you know?

About 17 million people visit London for a holiday every year. This is more than to any other UK city.

The town of Spa in Belgium gives its name to all towns where there are natural mineral waters.

Friends and neighbours

The people who live near you are called neighbours. Some of them become close friends. Sometimes they may also be your relatives. The small area near your home is the part of a **settlement** that you know best.

Housing estates

A town is made up of many different areas or districts. Most of these places are **residential** where there are mainly houses. A large area of housing is called a **housing estate**. A **suburb** is a housing area on the edge of a town or city.

A neighbourhood

The small area where people live is called a **neighbourhood**. People in a neighbourhood see each other almost daily. They are able to help each other when there are problems. Making friends with your neighbours and helping them is what goes to make a **community**.

In UK towns, there are Neighbourhood Watch groups to help prevent crime. Local people keep a special watch for strangers in their district.

A street fair in a new surburban housing estate in the UK.

Neighbours in this street have organized the event to help make a Local Community.

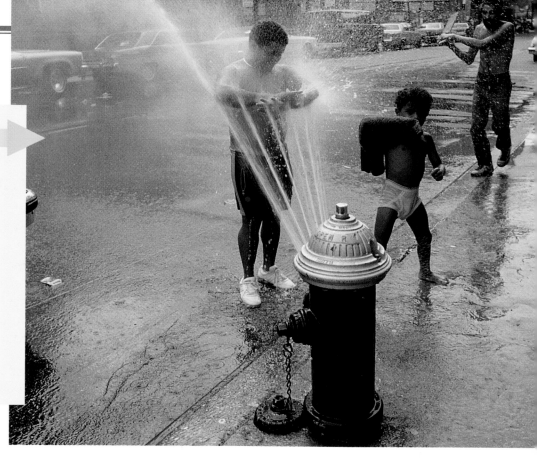

A street scene in Harlem, one of the poorer districts of New York City, USA.

People born in the area mix with others who have come from many different countries to form a community.

Neighbourhood facilities

A good neighbourhood has more than houses. It also needs a park and some play areas. Local shops are useful for buying things that are needed every day or when it is not possible to visit a larger shop.

A primary school is needed in places where there is a large number of young children. Young children need to be taken to and from school so the school should be near to where they live.

In some places, a church and church hall provide a place where people in a community can meet and do things together. Many neighbourhoods have purpose-built community centres.

Did you know?

There are 130,000 Neighbourhood Watch groups in the UK. These watch over about 5 million homes.

Many New Towns built in the UK since 1946 have small areas called neighbourhood units. About 3000 people live in each of these areas. The neighbourhood unit is a way that people can feel they are part of a small community, even in a big city.

Land for industry

In most towns and cities, some land is used for factories and **warehouses**. These are places where people earn a living by making and transporting goods. They can also affect the environment.

Factory land

In the past, factories were built near railways, docks and canals. These were the ways that **raw materials** and finished goods were transported. Houses were built alongside these factories so the workers would not have too far to walk to work.

Factory pollution

Living near these factories was unpleasant, and often unhealthy. Smoke from chimneys fell on buildings and made them turn black. People breathed in the **pollution** and became ill. For most factory owners, making a profit was more important than taking care of their workers' health and the environment.

Copsa Mica in Romania is said to be the world's most polluted town.

Air pollution from old factories is a serious health problem.

Modern industry in a suburban area.

Clean factories that do not cause pollution have been built near to roads. Trees and bushes hide some of the factories.

When a factory closes down, land is sometimes left **derelict**. It may be that the ground is too polluted with dangerous metal, such as lead, to be used for anything else.

Modern industry

Today, many of the old, dirty factories have closed down. Coal and steam engines have been replaced by electricity for power.

Also, factories are no longer built so close to houses. Instead, they are built on special areas called **industrial estates**. These are often near the edge of a city by a main road or motorway. Some are on inner city land where old factories used to be. By doing this, any noise and pollution from factories can be kept away from where people live.

Some places for industry are not just for factories. These are called **business parks**. Industries that pollute the environment are not allowed onto business parks.

Did you know?

A factory making nickel in the town of Nickel in Russia causes pollution by putting 250,000 tonnes of sulphur dioxide into the air every year.

Although very few factories in the UK still burn coal, about 80% of the electricity from power stations comes from burning coal, which pollutes the air.

Space for play

People need places to work, to relax and also for leisure. This is true for adults as well as for children. The type of play may be different, but the need for some **recreation** is the same. Space is needed for every type of recreation.

A playground

Each type of recreation needs a different amount of space. A small playground with slides and other pieces of equipment is all that is needed in a local neighbourhood.

Parks and city farms

A park is a larger area of land where people can go to relax and sometimes play a sport. In British cities, many of these were created during the last century. These are often laid out with flowers, trees and ornamental lakes.

A play space in central London.

It is hard to find safe play spaces for children in city centres.

The stadium used by the US baseball team, the Dodgers, in Los Angeles, California.

The pitch itself is only a small part of the space needed for a sports stadium.

There also needs to be seating and parking spaces.

In some towns, there are **city farms** where animals are reared for townspeople to visit. One of these is on the Isle of Dogs in London's old **dockland**.

Parks for nature

Some town parks are places where nature can be conserved. River banks and patches of derelict land can be used in this way.

A new idea in the UK is to plant a **forest park**. These are being planted on farmland near the edge of some cities.

Space for sport

Special places are needed for most types of sport. Golf courses take up a lot of space so these are usually on the edge of a town.

Other sports such as tennis and football need less space. A building called a stadium is built at a sports ground when a sport, such as football, is popular with spectators.

Did you know?

Some of the largest US sports stadiums have seats for over 100,000 spectators.

There are 35,000 accidents in UK playgrounds every year. It pays to be careful!

In the UK, there are less than two playgrounds for every 1000 children.

Shops and shopping

Every town and city is a centre for shopping. There are many types of shop, from small local shops to giant superstores. They are all in places where their customers can get to them most easily.

Local shops

It is handy to have a shopping centre near your home. A newsagent and somewhere to buy some basic foods may be all that is needed. A post office and a hairdresser can also provide useful local services. A small **neighbourhood** shopping centre usually has a range of shops for these daily needs.

City centre stores

Large shops are usually in a town centre. These sell a wide variety of goods at a range of prices. The largest town centre shops sell many different things and are called department stores. There are many smaller shops, called **specialist shops**, that only sell one type of product, such as shoes.

Many town centres have covered areas called **shopping malls**. These are safe from the weather and traffic. In some towns, streets are blocked off so pedestrians can walk from shop to shop in safety. This is called a **pedestrian precinct**.

The city centre of Chester.

There is a good range of shops and other services in this small, historic city.

The Merry Hill shopping area on the edge of Dudley in the West Midlands.

The shopping complex has nineteen car parks with space for 10,000 cars.

At the centre

The centre of a town is the most easily **accessible** area for most people. This is one reason why so many shops want to be there. A disadvantage is usually the lack of spaces for parking cars. It is hard to buy a lot then carry it all to a car park. Car parks can also be expensive to use.

Did you know?

In the UK, about 750 superstores have been built on the edge of towns and cities since 1986.

In the USA, so many shops and businesses in town centres have closed down that the centres are now called 'doughnuts' because there is nothing but a hole in the middle!

Out-of-town shopping

More people are now doing their shopping in supermarkets and in even larger **hypermarkets**. These are usually in shopping centres built outside of towns.

This type of shop takes up a very large amount of space. The buildings have to be on one floor because shopping is put into a trolley. It would be hard to wheel a trolley up and down several flights of stairs or move it in a lift.

The out-of-town centres are causing problems for other shops in a town. For example, in the UK, about 70% of business in Dudley's centre was lost since a new shopping area opened on the edge of the town.

High-rise cities

The tallest buildings are usually found in a city centre. Tall buildings are a way to make the most of the small amount of valuable land in a city centre.

Building skyscrapers

Tall buildings could not exist without a lift or an escalator. These were first put into buildings toward the end of the nineteenth century. By 1900, buildings more than 10 storeys high were being built in Chicago in the USA. Soon they were known as skyscrapers. Today, the Sears–Roebuck building in Chicago has 110 storeys.

The Central Business District

Most tall buildings are in a small area known as the **Central Business District** (CBD). Not many people live in the CBD. It is too noisy, there is too little space, and the cost of houses would be too high. Most of the buildings are shops and offices. In London, the area with most offices is called The City. Banks and insurance companies have headquarters there. It is a world centre for all types of business and **commerce**.

The Ginza district, one of the business districts in Tokyo, Japan.

Shops and offices that want to be in the centre all crowd together in tall buildings.

This is one of the busiest parts of Tokyo.

Public buildings

Public buildings such as law courts, government offices and a main library can also be found in a city centre. These are places that people from all over the city need to visit.

Day and night

The city centre is also a place for entertainment. There are cinemas and theatres, restaurants and night clubs. In the largest cities, something is going on 24 hours a day in the city centre.

The cost of land

The demand for space in a city centre means that the cost of land is high. As the cost of land goes up, it makes sense to build higher and higher. The same amount of ground space is needed for either a building that is one storey high, or one that is 101 storeys high.

Times Square in New York City.

There are theatres and other types of entertainment in this central part of the city.

Did you know?

The first working lift was put into a building in New York in 1859. The first moving staircase, or escalator, was built in 1900.

The tallest building in London is an office building called Canary Wharf. It is 750 feet high and has 50 storeys. Canary Wharf is in an area of old *dockland* that has been cleared and is now used for offices.

New life in dockland

Buildings do not last forever. They become old, rotten and even unsafe. Some old buildings are repaired because they are interesting. Others are knocked down and a new use is found for the land.

Change in the docks

In the past, sailing ships used to go as far up rivers as they could. They moored beside factories that were built to make flour from wheat, paper from wood and to make and repair ships. These areas became known as **dockland**. Networks of roads, canals and railways linked the docklands with other parts of the city and places further inland.

Closing the docks

But ships became longer, wider and needed deeper water. They could not get upstream to the old docks any more. New docks were built nearer the sea where goods could be moved using new methods and equipment. The new docks were away from the old city centre so lorries could get there more easily.

Without the ships, the old factories and **warehouses** soon closed down. Buildings were left empty and the land lay **derelict**. This is what happened to the old dockland areas in London, Liverpool, Bristol and other ports.

Old warehouses in Bristol's historic dockland near the centre of the city.

The docks were closed to cargo boats when ships became too big to get up the river Avon to the city.

Part of London's old dockland on the Isle of Dogs.

The Canary Wharf office block is the tallest building in the UK.

New ideas

But land in a city is never left unused for long. People soon had new ideas about how to use the old docklands. Giving a new use to a rundown area is called **urban redevelopment**.

Dockland's new look

In London's old docklands, water has been drained out of some of the docks. Now there are houses where ships used to dock. These houses are very popular because they are located close to where many people work.

The water in some docks has been kept for small pleasure boats and sports such as water skiing and sailing. Factories and warehouses have been knocked down. Now there are new offices, shops and restaurants.

There are some reminders of what the old dockland used to be like. Important historic buildings and some old cranes have been left.

Did you know?

London's old dockland along the river Thames stretches for 20 km downstream from St Katharine's dock by Tower Bridge.

Canary Wharf is linked to Tower Bridge by a computer-operated light railway that runs above ground.

Getting about

Add up the length of time you spend in a week getting from one place to another. It probably takes you several hours, no matter where you live.

The need to move

Living in a town is bound to mean you have to spend time travelling from place to place. Shops, school, parks and cinemas will all be in different places. Even your friends and relatives may not all live near each other.

Travel to work

One of the main reasons why people travel within a town is to go to work. Workers who have to travel some distance to work are called **commuters**. Their jobs may be in a town centre where there are large shops and offices, or in factories on **industrial estates** and **business parks**.

Commuters can spend several hours each day getting to and from work. Enormous traffic jams are caused as everyone tries to travel at the same time.

Travelling to work in Shanghai, China.

The most common way to travel in Chinese cities is by bicycle, even during the monsoon rains.

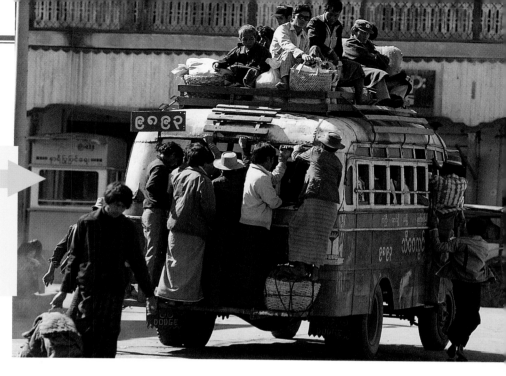

Travel by bus in a city in Burma. Safety takes second place to getting there!

Going by bike

Travelling in a city by bicycle can be as fast as travelling by car. Special cycle routes encourage more people to cycle and make it safer. Cycling is also a way of reducing the amount of air pollution and **traffic congestion**.

Did you know?

In China, there is one private car for every 2500 people. In the UK, there is one car for every three people.

In London, 43% of commuters travel to work by car. The figure for trains is 28%. In most UK cities, less than 2% of commuters travel by bicycle.

Public transport

A bus service is one type of **public transport**. Anybody can use it, provided they can pay the fare. But the bus route may not go exactly where you want to go, or at the right times.

One idea is to get people to '**park and ride**'. Cars are parked in special areas on the edge of town, and the rest of the journey is taken by bus. There are special bus-only lanes so that the bus is not held up by traffic. In the UK, cities such as Oxford, Bristol and Nottingham all have park and ride schemes.

Travel by car

For many people, travel by car is the most convenient way to get about. You can drive from door to door, at times that suit you best. But, large amounts of traffic cause many of the **pollution** problems in towns and cities today.

The traffic question

Networks of roads and streets connect different places in a town. Businesses in a town cannot work if people and goods cannot move easily from place to place. In towns and cities all over the world, it is getting harder to keep traffic moving.

Congested roads

The busiest roads are main roads that lead to a town's centre. Some of the traffic they carry goes to shops and offices in the centre. Some goes across the town from one **suburb** to another. These are the roads where there is most **traffic congestion**.

Traffic control

There are many ways to keep traffic moving safely. Traffic lights, roundabouts and 'one way' streets help to do this. Roads can be kept clear for traffic when parking is not allowed on them.

In Cambridge, cars have been fitted with a meter that records the length of time a car is stopped in a traffic jam. Drivers have to pay for the length of time they are stopped. The aim of this is to reduce the number of cars trying to get into the city.

A shopping centre in Hounslow, West London.

Traffic lights control traffic at this busy junction. Double yellow lines mean parking is not allowed.

Railings keep pedestrians safe and off the roads.

Freeways in Los Angeles, California.

There are 3 million vehicles on the roads every day in Los Angeles.

New roads

The most expensive solution to traffic problems is to build an **urban motorway**. This solves the problem in one place, but can move it on to somewhere else.

A **ring road** or **by-pass** takes traffic away from a town centre. This is useful for drivers who are only travelling through the centre. With less traffic, life is made better for people who live in the town. Others who have to live near the new ring road are not always so happy. They have to put up with the noise and **pollution** from the new road.

The M25 lesson

The M25 motorway was built as a ring road around London. It was supposed to help traffic flow more freely. Now it is one of the city's most congested roads because it has attracted more drivers to use it.

There were plans to widen the M25 motorway from six lanes to fourteen lanes, but there have been many objections. Perhaps other answers need to be found to the growing problems caused by urban traffic.

Did you know?

There are 5000 new vehicles on the roads in the UK every day.

There are 4000 deaths on UK roads every year.

If the traffic in a city comes to a complete standstill, there will be *gridlock*.

Track travel

It is hard to get anywhere on time with so many people using the roads. There has to be an answer to this. One answer is for more people to travel by **public transport**.

Train travel

Travel by train is one option. Trains can travel quickly because nothing gets in their way. The only time they stop is so that passengers can get on and off or at signals while they wait for other trains.

The Moscow subway was opened in 1935.

About 4 million passengers travel on the subway every day. It is one of the world's fastest and cleanest underground systems.

Commuters into some of the world's largest cities, such as Tokyo and London, often travel for over an hour each day on a train to work.

Go underground

In 1863, the world's first underground railway line was opened in London. Since then, underground railways have been built in other big cities. The Metro in Paris and Moscow and the New York Subway are three of these.

Nothing can get in the way of an underground train. The problem is that not everyone lives near an underground station.

The monorail in Sydney, the largest city in Australia.

The monorail track takes passengers quickly and safely around the central area of Sydney.

City trams

In some cities such as Manchester, trams run on their own tracks on the roads. Like a bus, trams are able to carry a large number of people at once. They take up far less space than the same number of people driving cars. A vehicle that does this is called a **mass transit system**.

Rapid transit

There are many other ways to carry a large number of people quickly. These are called **rapid transit systems**.

A monorail is one way to do this. A special track has to be built above the level of the streets. One of these has been built in Sydney, the largest city in Australia.

Modern rapid transit systems cause little **pollution** and help take cars off the roads. More and more cities are building systems like these.

Did you know?

A light railway was opened in Manchester in 1992. Now it carries 13 million passengers each year. Almost half the passengers used to travel by car.

There are new rapid transit lines in some cities in the USA such as St Louis and San Francisco.

Sea ports and airports

Most big cities are linked to other big cities by a **sea port** or an airport, often both. These are places where **freight** and passengers are moved. They help put a city on the international map.

Port city

Some of the world's largest cities are also sea ports. These ports **import** and **export** freight that is heavy and bulky.

Ships bring different kinds of work that help a city to grow. Dock workers, customs officers, lorry drivers and many others are all needed. In some cities such as Hamburg in Germany, thousands of people work in **shipyards**.

Near the port, goods are made in factories. Paper is made from wood and petrol is made from crude oil. Goods are stored in **warehouses**. There are more jobs in banks and insurance companies to handle the financial and **administration** side of the shipping business.

Special ports

Some towns have a special type of port. These are the naval towns such as Plymouth in the UK and San Diego in the USA. They are the home bases for navy warships. There are ferry ports such as Dover in England and Calais in France. Ferry boats make regular crossings between these ports.

The port of Rotterdam in The Netherlands is mainly for freight such as crude oil and iron ore.

A new port for Rotterdam called Europoort has been built nearer to the North Sea.

Tampa International Airport in Florida, USA.

Passengers come to Florida on business and to visit the state's many tourist attractions.

Aircraft fly low over houses near the airport.

Travel by air

Millions of people pass through **domestic** and **international** airports every year. Domestic flights are those that start and finish inside the same country. For example, a flight from New York to Chicago in the USA is a domestic flight. International flights are between different countries, for example, from Sydney to New York.

Did you know?

About 114 million people use UK airports each year. This is two times for every person in the UK.

The world's busiest airport is O'Hare Airport in Chicago, USA. About 60 million passengers travel through it every year.

Airport city

An airport is like a small town in some ways. Some are actually bigger than many small towns. A runway can be over 4 km long with the whole airport taking up to 20 km^2.

There are shops, car parks and restaurants. Hotels and factories are sometimes built near major airports. At least 50,000 people depend on London's Heathrow Airport for their jobs.

A noisy neighbour

Not many people want to live near an airport because of aircraft noise. There is also the risk of an accident near an airport. Most aircraft accidents are during take-off and landing. In spite of these problems, no major city can afford to be without an airport.

The new English village

Old villages and small country towns in England can look very attractive. Cottages, old churches and nearby countryside are more appealing than the houses, roads and factories in a town. These are also called **rural** areas.

New homes

The most popular villages are near to the towns and cities. A problem is that there are not enough houses in villages to meet the demand from people who want to live there.

One answer is to change old buildings such as barns into houses. Another answer is to build new houses. It is not easy to build new houses so that they do not ruin the look of an old village. If too many houses are built, then the village becomes the size of a town.

Village houses are often expensive to buy. The prices go up because the people who move there are usually **commuters** with well-paid jobs. A village like this is called a **dormitory village**.

A village post office in Gloucestershire, UK.

A small number of tourists in this village help keep the village shops open.

New houses in a village about 10 miles from Southampton.

These were built for commuters who work in nearby towns.

Losing shops and services

In the past, village people used to do their shopping in a village shop. Now three out of every four drive to a town superstore. This can mean that village shops have to close down.

Bus services do not come to a village very often. This makes it hard for people who do not own a car to do their shopping.

Other village services such as small village schools have been closed down. It costs less for each pupil in a larger school. It is hard for parents to take their children to school in another village or town and collect them again.

Saving the village

In some villages, the shops and schools have been saved by the new people moving in. Extra facilities have been built such as community centres. Not all the changes have been bad.

Did you know?

In the UK, about 20% of the people live in the countryside. Most of these live in villages.

In rural areas of the UK, one in eight households does not have a car.

In the UK, there were 4300 schools with under 1000 pupils in 1974. By 1994, there were only 3200.

Building up, building out

Parts of a town are always changing. Buildings that become old and unsafe may have to be knocked down. In other places, new buildings are put up.

Inner city change

Towns and cities grow outwards from their first site. This means that the oldest parts are always near the centre. This is where the most improvement may be needed.

In the UK and USA, an old inner city district is sometimes called a **'twilight zone'**. The residential population in most of these areas has gone down over the last 50 years.

Some old buildings, factories or houses are best demolished. Demolition clears the land for new houses and other types of land use. Making improvements to these areas is called **urban renewal**.

Demolition of an old building near the centre of a city.

Explosives are carefully placed to make sure the building collapses on itself.

The city's edge

New houses, factories, shops and roads are also built on the edge of cities. **Housing estates** now sprawl across land that used to be green fields.

Protecting farmland

Some farmland around cities is being protected by laws that do not allow new building. This is done by making a **green belt** around the city.

A green belt gives townspeople some open space to look at and walk through. It also stops the **suburbs** of one city from reaching the suburbs of another, leaving no green space between them.

A problem is that a green belt does not always stop the growth. Farmland is protected but new buildings are built on land that is even further out of the city.

A new housing estate on the edge of Brighton.

The population in nearby rural districts has gone up as more people have moved out of the local town and in from other towns.

Did you know?

Green belts were first put around cities in the UK in 1938.

The population of Brighton in East Sussex went down by 20,000 between 1961 and 1991. In one *rural* district near Brighton, the population went up by 30,000 over the same time.

An urban world

A group of Masai cattle herders in Kenya.

The men are celebrating building a new village. They have to move from place to place in search of grass.

Some of these men may become migrants to Nairobi and other towns.

It is hard to know what to do when you have two choices and both of them are bad. This is what faces millions of people in some of the world's poorest countries.

Life on the land

Most people in the world's poorest countries live in villages. They have a difficult life working on farms. Many work for someone else as labourers. Their pay is low and they can often only work for a few months each year.

Many farm owners are not much better off. They own so little land that it is hard to grow enough food to live on.

Living in a village

Living in a village in the developing world has other problems. Water often has to be fetched from a well or river. Sometimes it is muddy, polluted and a danger to health. The nearest doctor or clinic may be many kilometres away in a town. There is little choice of jobs, even when children pass their exams.

Moving to the city

Millions of people in the world's poor countries are leaving the countryside and moving to the cities. These people are called **migrants**. The move to the towns is called **urbanization**.

A better chance

The 'push' from the countryside is easy to understand. The 'pull' of the cities is also easy to see. Rich people live in the cities. There may be regular work in a city factory.

There are schools, hospitals and cinemas in the cities. It may take some time to get a job and become more wealthy. At least the chance of doing so is better in the city.

These are some of the reasons why so many people are deciding to move to a city. It also helps explain why some cities are growing so quickly.

People from the countryside building their own homes on the edge of Nairobi, Kenya.

The population of Nairobi was about 350,000 in 1970. By 1986, it had risen to about 1,500,000. Since then, it has carried on increasing.

Did you know?

In 1980, New York was the world's largest city with 16 million people.

By the year 2000, Mexico City will be the world's largest city with over 30 million people.

Divided people

Cities are where the greatest differences in people's wealth can be seen side by side.

Homes for the poor

For poor people, the same street scenes can be seen in most of the world's developing countries. There are **slum** areas where some of the poorest people live crowded together in old, rundown buildings. There are also people whose only home is the street.

Shanty towns

Some poor people live in homes they have built for themselves. These are usually in large areas called **shanty towns**.

Shanty towns are often built on land that is unsafe because it is too steep, or unhealthy because of disease, or danger from floods. They are often built illegally on land the people do not own. Shanty towns are called 'barongays' in the Philippines, 'bustees' in India and 'favelas' or 'barrios' in South America.

Rio de Janeiro, one of the largest cities in Brazil.

Many of the people in Rio de Janeiro are very wealthy. The wealth helps attract more people, some very poor, to the city.

Rich lifestyles

Rich people in the cities of the developing world have a very different way of life. Some work in offices for big companies or for the government. They live in well-built houses and blocks of flats.

Their homes are often protected by high fences and armed guards or dogs. There is a real fear that they might be robbed by people who have nothing. Jobs such as cooking, cleaning and looking after children are done by maids and other servants.

Getting better

There is no quick way that poor people can improve their living conditions. Wages stay low as long as there are so many people looking for a job.

Some shanty towns in Lima, the capital city of Peru, are now more than 30 years old. There are shops, banks, health facilities and schools. Many people have steady jobs and have been able to improve their homes. The city council has also built new homes as well as providing water supplies, drains and electricity.

Did you know?

By the year 2000, eight out of the world's top ten biggest cities will be in the world's poorest countries.

The chief city minister of Delhi in India has said that 'By the year 2001, Delhi will be the world's biggest slum'. The city population is increasing by 600,000 every year.

Shanty town houses have been built up the steep slopes of Rio de Janeiro in Brazil.

Heavy rain causes avalanches that can destroy these homes.

Life on the edge

Cities are some of the most unsafe places on Earth. There are more crimes, traffic accidents and health problems in cities than in most other places. Some cities have even been built in places that make them unsafe.

Natural hazards

Some risks are from natural disasters such as earthquakes and floods. Many people live in major cities where earthquakes are common. In San Francisco, Tokyo and Mexico City, earthquakes in the past have killed thousands of people and left others homeless. Floods are a problem in cities by rivers such as Dhaka in Bangladesh and Cologne in Germany.

There are also cities such as Miami in Florida that are hit by hurricanes. People need to be prepared for these kinds of risks.

Watch out!

Crime in cities is a very different kind of risk. The amount of crime in some districts is more than in others. People who live in the poorest districts are more likely to suffer from crime than in richer districts. In all **neighbourhoods**, everyone needs to make sure that opportunities for crime are kept low.

Diseases have always spread quickly in towns and cities. This is because so many people live close together.

A scene in Los Angeles, California, USA.

The police are searching young people for illegal drugs.

Many crimes are caused by people trying to get enough money to buy drugs.

People sharing a dirty water supply can quickly be infected with diseases such as cholera. This is why it is so important to have proper drains and a clean water supply.

There are also health problems from car and factory **pollution**. Simply breathing in city air can be a health risk.

Did you know?

An earthquake in 1988 killed 20,000 people in Mexico City. One thousand people were killed when one block of flats collapsed.

People sleeping rough in London.

At least 300 people sleep like this in London every night.

Homeless and hopeless

A growing number of people in both rich and poor countries are without a job. It is hard to have a home without a job. It is also hard to get a job without having a home.

Even in wealthy cities such as London, there are about 50,000 homeless people. Most live in temporary accommodation but at least 300 sleep in doorways and **derelict** buildings every night.

Future cities

Many of the people who will be living in the year 2020 have already been born. The same towns and cities will still exist, but how will they be different from today?

Growing cities

One difference is that most cities will be much bigger with more people living in them. Most of the biggest cities will be in the world's poorest countries.

One reason is that there will be nearly twice as many people on the Earth. The second is because more people will have moved from the countryside to find work in the cities.

In the richer countries, cities will get bigger as more people move out to the edge. Nearby **rural** areas will become part of the city.

New architecture

Some historic buildings will still be there but many of today's buildings will have been demolished. Perhaps your house will not be there. **Architects** will have designed new buildings and changed the look of some parts of the city landscape.

La Defense, an office and housing area in Paris, France.

Architects will have new ideas about how buildings should look.

New building materials with new shapes and colours could be used in the future.

Poor people's self-built houses alongside rich people's houses in Nairobi, Kenya.

Scenes such as this could still be common in the year 2020.

Transport 2020

In Europe and North America, there could be twice as many cars and lorries on the roads by the year 2020. More roads and car parks will be needed unless there is more and better public transport that people will use. Pollution from cars and lorries must be reduced if people are to be healthy.

Cyber city

There will be more computers in offices and also in people's homes. More people will work from home. People will make new friends on the worldwide computer networks like the **Internet**. Computers and cameras will help control crime.

Traffic will be controlled by computers, though it may not flow any faster. Shopping could be done by **virtual reality** without the need to walk around a shop.

A future for everyone

The biggest question about the future has to be about people's standard of living. Bigger cities will need more homes, more jobs and more services such as water, power and sewerage. Far more effort will need to be put into making sure that everyone has a share in the world's wealth.

Did you know?

The world population in 1995 was about 5 billion. By the year 2020, it could be over 8 billion.

Glossary

accessible a place where people can get to easily

administration organizing people

architects people whose job is to design buildings

business parks land that is specially for factories, offices and other businesses

by-pass a road taking traffic away from a busy town or city

capital city the city where a country has its government

Central Business District an area in the centre of a city for shops and offices

charter a document that gave permission to hold a market

city farms a farm in a city mainly for recreation and education

civil servants people who work on government business

coalfield an area where there is coal

commerce different types of business

community the people who live near each other

commuters people who travel some distance to their work every day

derelict land or buildings that are left unused and ruined

dockland the land around a harbour for industry and warehouses

domestic (airport) for flights inside a country

dormitory village a village for commuters

export to send goods out of a country

forest parks areas of forest on the edge of a city

freight goods

ghost towns settlements that have been abandoned

government the people who rule a country

greenbelt land around cities where building is not allowed

gridlock when traffic in a city comes to a complete standstill

hamlet a very small settlement with only a few houses

housing estate a large area of houses

hypermarkets very large supermarkets

import to bring goods into a country

industrial estates land that is specially for factories

industrial town a town where many people work in factories

international (airport) for flights between different countries

Internet a network of links between computers

isolated settlement a single settlement on its own

location where a place is situated

manufacturing industry making goods in factories

mass transit system public transport vehicles that carry a lot of people

migrants people who have left their home and moved to live in another part of a country

mineral a rock that can be used as a resource

Ministries departments in a government such as Environment, Defence and Education

neighbourhood a small area where people live

nomads people who move their home from place to place

park and ride a scheme to encourage motorists to park their cars then use public transport

pedestrian precincts shopping areas where traffic is kept out

politician a person who represents people and makes political decisions

pollution harmful substances in the air or water supply

public buildings buildings such as libraries, law courts and hospitals that are for everyone to use

public transport a vehicle that anyone who pays can use

rapid transit system public transport vehicles that travel quickly

raw materials the natural materials used to make goods from

recreation play activities

residential where people live

resort a settlement used by holidaymakers

ring road a road going around a busy town or city

rural to do with the countryside

settlement a place where people always live

shanty towns areas on the edge of a city where people have built their own home

shipyards places where ships are built and repaired

shopping malls covered areas for shops

slum old, crowded and decaying buildings in a city

spa towns towns where there are natural mineral waters

specialist shops shops that have only one type of product

subsistence farming growing food to feed a farming family

suburb houses towards the edge of a city

tourist industry the business of providing holiday transport, accommodation and other facilities

traders people who buy and sell goods

traffic congestion when traffic becomes too much to move freely

twilight zone the old inner area of a city

urban development changing part of a city

urban motorway a motorway through an urban area

urban renewal to rebuild part of a town

urbanization more people moving to live in towns and cities

virtual reality to make places or things seem real on a computer screen

warehouses buildings to store freight

Index

Numbers in plain type (32) refer to the text; numbers in italic (*33*) refer to a caption.